THE COLOUR OF SAYING

The Colour of Saying

THE WORK OF MARY LLOYD JONES   edited by Eve Ropek

GOMER PRESS
with Aberystwyth Arts Centre

First impression 2001

ISBN 1 85902 869 1

Designed by Elgan Davies.

Cover illustration: detail from installation.
Cover photograph of Mary Lloyd Jones by Tina Carr.

All photographs of paintings by Tina Carr except on pages 57, 60, 64, 65, 69, 71, 78, 94, 105, 106 and 113 (Huw Gwilliam) and pages 25, 58 and 92 (Graham Matthews).

The publishers gratefully acknowledge the financial support of the Arts Council of Wales towards the commissioning of one of the articles.

This book is published in association with Aberystwyth Arts Centre.

Printed in Wales at Gomer Press, Llandysul, Ceredigion.

contents

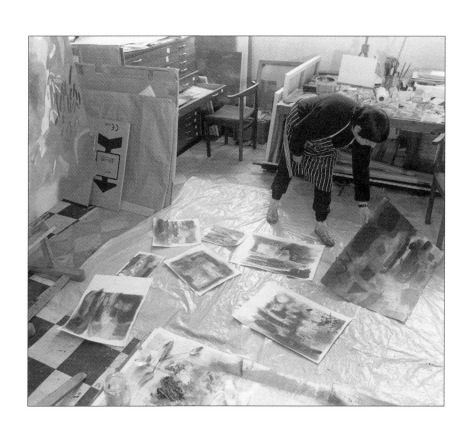

Introduction *Eve Ropek*

This volume is a timely celebration of an artist at the height of her powers. Mary Lloyd Jones's work is mature, with the visual subtlety and developed personal language only achieved by years of pursuing the right visual expression; yet she remains ceaselessly exploratory within her chosen field.

Her choice of subject matter is the landscape, most often that around her home in Ceredigion. The landscape of Wales has inspired artists – both home-grown and imported – for centuries: Richard Wilson, Turner, Graham Sutherland, John Piper, Augustus and Gwen John, even Stanley Spencer (who pushed his pram laden with paints and equipment through the countryside), David Nash and Kyffin Williams. All these and legions more have seen with clarity, and attempted to interpret, Wales's dramatic landscapes; that changeable, sylvan countryside with extremes ranging from high craggy mountains, to rolling hills, to sheltered coves – an ancient land full of Neolithic and Celtic remains.

The most successful landscape art, however, achieves more than simply a reproduction in paint of an outward appearance. Mary Lloyd Jones's paintings incorporate a knowledge of the history, social and geographic, of her country. Her work attempts a distillation of the landscape, seeks to capture its physical being, complete with scars, while revealing its history and – curiously, in works from which the human figure is always absent – showing our relationship to the land past and present. 'True being' in Mary Lloyd Jones's paintings is simultaneously the appearance of things seen and the spiritual and historical reality of it. When asked to define art, the Eskimo artist Kenoujuak said: 'It is simply to transfer one's vision from the real to the unreal'. Mary Lloyd Jones makes this transition in her paintings seem easy.

Paintings are also about canvas, calico, dyes, paint and pencil marks: the physical reality of Mary's work is at one with her vision of the land. Vivid unsubdued colour, sweeping marks and an evident delight in the application of paint allow the viewer to enter into the artist's way of seeing. It is possible to visualise the paintings being made, to separate, as one observes them, the layers and marks of paint – much as Mary Lloyd Jones herself unveils the history of the hills she sees and learns about. Studies are painted exploratively for the joy of the moment, with a freedom to explore and take risks. These may contain the germ of an idea for a larger painting, which may then be kept to one side for the future.

What has influenced Mary? This question will be answered fully in the following essays, but briefly this artist's life has embraced a wide sphere of influences. Brought up simply, in a rural area, the landscape was simply part of her and therefore not to be remarked upon. A traditional art school education introduced all the taught elements, good and bad, common to most twentieth-century artists. A brave self-knowledge brought her home, to Wales, where her vision developed. From her base, influences of contemporary culture from all over this well-connected world have continually fed her interests; from America to India, Mary continues to be open to learning.

Before photography, painters would help people to see and to love their land; today, we have an enormous amount of visual information of every sort, and our needs are different. Yet inspirational art of and about the land in which we live remains vital. A hugely important part of Mary Lloyd Jones's life, and thus her work, is her sense of belonging to an ethnic group which until relatively recently was denied a proper respect in its own country. As a Welsh speaker who was brought up in the Welsh rural tradition, she delights in being part of the new Wales where a distinctly Welsh 'take' on history, on art and on life is consciously being sought and published, transmitted and talked about. This is indeed, in 2001, an exciting time for the arts scene in Wales: the old ways of doing things hang in the balance. This is a time full of potential, of pride in Welsh achievements, accompanied by an upsurge of creativity. There is a feeling of rediscovery, a sense of pride of place, of pride in the artists of Wales. Welsh artists have achieved a greater resonance and cultural significance within their culture as people re-think the past. Museums and galleries are reconsidering their displays and collections. Galleries, museums, art dealers and collectors within the art world are extremely powerful and influential, in that they tend to share certain assumptions about art and culture, and as Noam Chomsky has pointed out: 'they . . . undertake to analyse and present some picture of social reality . . . they create the ideological justification for social practice'.

There is nothing sinister about this, but we can expect to see real change in a society's attitudes to art and culture when the spotlight shines fully on an alternative history. This is not to forget that artists of Wales are also inevitably, and thankfully, part of the greater tide of British and European cultural expression, and that they are constantly contributing to it and learning from it.

The accepted artistic 'tradition' is inevitably selective in terms of both a 'London-centric' bias, and a patriarchal viewpoint. Of course, no history or criticism can exist without some sort of selection. Raymond Williams himself has noted that

> *always selectivity is the point; the way in which from a whole area of past and present, certain meanings and practices are chosen for emphasis, certain other meanings and practices are excluded.*

Pursuing this a little further, it is clear that another important aspect of Mary Lloyd Jones's work is that she is *she*, not *he*. Women's lives have opened out enormously in recent years but no one could yet argue that life offers them a level playing field. Traditionally art made by women has been regarded less highly than that of male artists; effectively,

Installation, Side 14

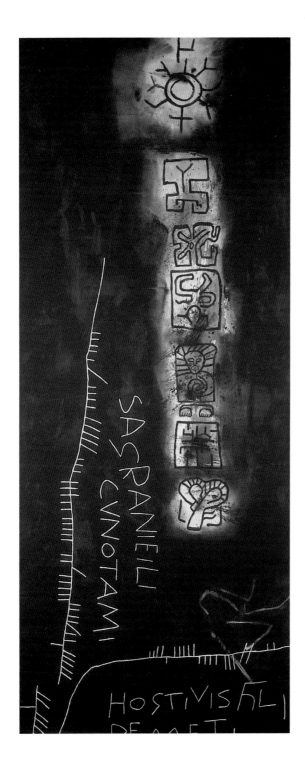

Installation, Side 3

women's artistic expression has been continually erased by the 'tradition' as officially validated through the common consensus of the art world. The oil painting, for example, has continued to hold connotations of superiority, an aura of intrinsically special value. Mary Lloyd Jones's work evolved in the early 1980s to take the form of large irregularly shaped paintings, which were unstretched. This was an exciting development in her work, which led to her making her mark in a spectacularly effective way. Yet this work failed to achieve commercial success, and its links with female achievements – cloth, stitching, dye soaking into the cloth – seemed a drawback to many people rather than the positive connection with femininity as which it might be perceived. Mary's work moved on past this period to rediscover the traditional forms of painting again; but, had the art world been prepared at the time to acknowledge a broader range of work, her output of this period would have achieved greater recognition for the breakthrough which it heralded.

This book is published to coincide with a large exhibition of new work by Mary Lloyd Jones in Gallery 1, at the newly extended Aberystwyth Arts Centre. As part of her show, Mary has made ten large free-hanging paintings, hung to articulate the space of the twenty-foot high gallery with its curved ceiling. These works return to some of the techniques of the large free-hanging paintings of the eighties, combined with the use of proclamatory banners. They

Installation detail, Side 10

incorporate her love of the poetry of Wales, its indigenous language, and its landscape, within a sequence which travels through time from prehistory to the present.

In the essays in this book, each contributor illuminates different facets of Mary Lloyd Jones's art. Nigel Jenkins considers the roots of her work and early life in Wales; Mary Sara sets the work in the context of art history; Derek Hyatt offers a vivid personal viewpoint, a guide for the viewer; Peter Abbs applauds the humanity of the work; Gillian Clarke combines both prose and poetry in response to the artist's paintings and the Welsh landscape; and Mary herself has written a short piece on her life and work.

As Mary Sara points out in her essay, once you have been drawn into Mary Lloyd Jones's work, the journey through the Welsh landscape becomes a different experience, as if seen through her eyes. Those colours, so vivid, are actually there to be seen; the symbols and scars, they too can be experienced in the folds and heights of the hills. As Frank Stella has remarked:

The idea of being a painter is to declare an identity. Not just my identity, an identity for me, but an identity big enough for everyone to share. Isn't that what it's all about?

Mary Lloyd Jones has forged an identity, a big enough identity; she has given us a new way of seeing the landscape about us, and for this we are grateful.

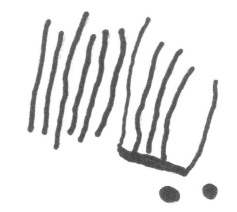

Singing the Landscape *Nigel Jenkins*

When they asked her in school what she wanted to be when she grew up, the little girl from Pontarfynach had no doubt about the answer: an artist. But she dared not voice it. Mary Lloyd Jones knew, even at the age of seven, that hers was a laughably outlandish ambition, so, to avoid the guffaws of her classmates, she offered up some suitably demure alternative, and kept her dreams to herself.

Inevitably, she found herself performing a range of life's more conventional roles, not least those of housewife, mother and teacher, but she remained doggedly true to that first desire. Mary Lloyd Jones is today one of Wales's most adventurous and provocative landscape artists, a passionate symphonist in colour, whose works in a wide variety of media – luminous watercolours, battlesome oils, calico works of formidable scale and beauty – are in demand through the countries of Britain, mainland Europe and the USA.

So many of 'our' painters either fled the nest early, seldom to return (the Richard Wilson trajectory) or, like Graham Sutherland, flew in, already well plumaged, from the big nest next door. Of the hundreds of artists at work in Wales today, a minority, I'd guess, are native-born, and many, finding Wales too hard to handle, have exiled themselves internally from their cultural context. Mary Lloyd Jones is a comparative rarity – a Welsh-born artist, a woman of *y fro Gymraeg* (Welsh-speaking Wales), who has stood her ground in Wales, engaging all the more profoundly for it with the topography, history, folk life and languages of her country as her art has matured.

Welsh artists are sometimes warned off landscape painting. It is said to be an alien form, an English import; there were never the patrons in poverty-stricken Wales to foster the growth of an indigenous landscape tradition; Welsh artists would make more patriotic use of their time and talent reconfecting the *gwerin* or carving lovespoons. The trouble with this argument is that it neglects a centuries-old landscape tradition that is undeniably indigenous: that of the poets. The spirit of place has moved consistently through Welsh poetry, from the *cynfeirdd* down to modern poets such as Waldo Williams eulogising the Preseli Hills or, in English, Chris Torrance, remembrancer of Cwm Nedd. It is a tradition not simply of surfaces, as in photographic views, but of depths and contested meanings. If permission is sought by the contemporary visual artist, here, surely, it is to be found. Mary Lloyd Jones, who often uses words or lines of poetry in her paintings, draws evident strength from her country's literary treasure-trove, although she, like many other visual artists, must wish sometimes that a modest fraction of the adulation heaped upon Wales's poets might tiptoe now and then in the direction of Wales's relatively neglected painters.

Most neatly representational landscapes seem to issue from a world that is anchored in the solidities of classical Newtonian mechanics: what the eye sees is what the hand attempts to paint. The modern artist, alert to the consequences of quantum mechanics, relativity and chaos theory, and conscious of the findings of archaeologists and anthropologists, knows that there is more to all this than meets the eye. The old strategies for pinning down visual images – perspective, due proportion, colour – are incapable of articulating the complex phenomena with which an artist such as Mary Lloyd Jones might wish to engage. She has had to find a new means of expression, although her main subject, upland mid and west Wales, is at least 440 million years old. Humankind was not even an itch in the amphibian skull when these mountains pushed up into their primordial shape; and doubtless, given the speed with which we seem intent on burning ourselves out, they'll weather back down without us too. It is between these poles that Mary Lloyd Jones's art moves, celebrating all the energies – geological, vegetable, animal, human – that have made her landscape what it is, and warning, long before the 'green' tag became fashionable, of the dangers of human alienation from the Earth. 'My aim,' she says, 'is not to reproduce outward appearances but to attempt to convey the spirit of a particular place. Through my work I try to create links with the past, to the lives of previous generations, to folk memory and to the myths and legends, all of which contribute to the atmosphere of a landscape. I would like to bring about a heightened awareness of the land and the multi-faceted nature of our understanding of it.'

She may have known from an early age that she wanted to be an artist, but it took Mary Lloyd Jones several decades to realise that her most rewarding subject would be the hills and valleys of her native *bro*, a choppy swathe of Ceredigion which might look today like the epitome of 'rural Wales' but which is one of the earliest sites of industrial despoliation in Britain, thanks to the lead and silver mining that was pursued here from the time of the Romans. Pontarfynach (Devil's Bridge), twelve miles east of Aberystwyth, gave her a warm and encouraging childhood, but artists were unheard-of creatures there, and Mary felt, as she grew up, that she would have to get away in order to become one. It's only since the 1980s that she has managed to 'come home', mining in the Ystwyth and Rheidol valleys an apparently inexhaustible seam of inspiration, and finding in herself the confidence to paint not as she 'ought' to but as she needs.

She was born in 1934 into a family of farmers and wool workers rooted, for as long as they remember, in the region of Pumlumon; she is sure she is of pre-Celtic stock. Theirs, she says, was a traditional peasant way of life, though there were books, newspapers and fiery discussions; her father was a wonderful storyteller.

'I was forever drawing,' she told me, 'and my parents gave me every encouragement. My brother was born when I was three, but there were no other kids around at all. I had to amuse myself. Drawing was my great entertainment.' Although steeped in all the nuances of twentieth-century Modernism, she seems never to have lost sight of the spontaneity and magic of childhood creativity. 'In a world dominated by Cartesian rationality and masculine logic, where only that which is measurable is given value, I wish to demonstrate through creative endeavour the importance of intuition, of lateral and irrational thought processes. Logic is not enough, and in our imbalanced culture to seek out that which is immeasurable is important.' Tapping such forces, she works powerful transformations.

On the daily trip to Ardwyn Grammar School in Aberystwyth, Mary would pass by the landscape which, to the mature artist, would become something of an obsession; to her, then, it meant nothing – just so much wind-blown grass. She had heard jazz on the radio, and was eager to escape to the alluringly alien planet from which that tantalising music appeared to come.

Cardiff Art School, which she entered in 1951, seemed indeed a galaxy away from the rural solitudes of Ceredigion. Lodging at Tonpentre, Mary would travel down to the city on the Rhondda train: 'I was shocked. Everything was so bleak, so black and filthy and awful, and I couldn't understand why nobody else seemed to be shocked. Cardiff was a terrific culture shock initially, but I was chuffed to be in the city and absorbed everything madly.'

The college course fell somewhat short of expectations, and it was in the company of fellow students, headed by the stellar Ernest Zobole (1927-99), that Mary gained most of her education. 'Every day we'd take over a compartment on the Rhondda train and have intense discussions going down to Cardiff. If anyone was foolish enough to come into our compartment it was arranged that someone would throw a fit, and the intruder would soon absent himself from our manic seminar.' There would be sandwiches in the park at lunchtime, then a session with the art books in the Central Library or a visit to the National Museum's Gwendoline Davies Collection; the Impressionists exerted an irresistible pull.

So too did Rhondda-born John Jones, a student in the same year as Mary. They married towards the end of the course, and, after John's national service, left Wales for him to take a teaching job in Romford. There had been little discussion, in the ferment of the Cardiff years, of what it might mean to be a 'Welsh artist'; indeed, the words seemed to cancel each other out. 'In order to be a painter I had not to be Welsh, I thought. We felt we had been missing out by not being near London. That, we thought, was the place to be, so we were keen to make the move.' Their first daughter, Gudrun, was eleven months old; their second, Sianed, was born the following year, in 1959. They stayed three years altogether, but it was hardly the promised land of their imaginings, and they came back home every holiday, 'to keep sane'.

In 1961 they managed to return to Wales for good, settling in the Aberaeron area initially, and making a living as teachers in various schools and art colleges. In 1975 they bought an old school in Aberbanc near Llandysul, and

Jets

converted it into a comfortable home with spacious studios and residential facilities for small groups of students. They were for many years a mystery tour destination for the W.I. and Merched y Wawr. Fifty at a time would troop into Mary's studio for perhaps their first confrontation with modern art.

To the fan of chocolate-box scenes, Mary Lloyd Jones's work must look as if someone has gone crazy with a paint palette. She likes to help the sceptical viewer to a deeper understanding of her art by pointing to connections between her uncompromisingly contemporary works, with their abstracting tendencies, and the often entirely abstract design of something as cosily familiar as the traditional patchwork quilt. It was a revelation for her when, in the early seventies, her aunt dug out an old quilt made by Mary's great-grandmother. 'Here was a woman artist using colour and form in an abstract, confident and emotional way, producing a large-scale and public piece of art.' The quilt, hung proudly in Mary's living room, was the permission for which her imagination had been waiting.

On the wall opposite is a deeply affecting portrait of her father which, painted in 1973, represents another significant advance, moving her on from experiments in geometrical abstraction towards an art that, still formally daring, concerns itself more centrally with the artist's own people, places and preoccupations. It was much praised in the 1974 National Eisteddfod. 'I like to have it around,' she jokes, 'because it shows people who are baffled by my squiggles that I *can* do "the real thing".'

Like Iolo Morganwg, that mercurial genius of the eighteenth century, she is a remembrancer, a praise-poet in oils and watercolours of the layered history and numinous forces of the land of Wales. 'The real thing', surface reality imitated in pseudo-photographic terms, is of no interest to Mary Lloyd Jones. Hers is a spirited, intuitive art in rebellion against stodgy academicism and the Sunday painter's fussing over authenticating detail. We are offered an inhabited, worked-over, ever-changing landscape, rather than 'scenery' which, innocent of human toil, is merely 'beautiful'. Like much Welsh poetry, her paintings have that rare ability to function both abstractly – as 'objects in themselves' – and as interpretations of specific and recognisable places. She talks of her attempt to honour the spirit of place as 'singing the landscape'. Hers is a considerable responsibility, for, having encountered the work of Mary Lloyd

Jones, we are unlikely ever again to see the Welsh landscape as we did before: she broadens and deepens our understanding.

'A painting *starts* with what I see, but what happens on the canvas or on the cloth is something else. At Ponterwyd, for instance, I found some quartz scattered in a certain shape on the hillside, and this suggested markings of a more human kind. When I worked up the painting from a number of small sketches I made on the spot, I deliberately emphasised and simplified those shapes. To give another example, the felling of the forestry is noisy and brutal, and the ground is left looking much like a battlefield. In my paintings I choose to use colour expressively. Red is the colour of blood, and my paintings show a land hacked and bruised, exposing raw and scarred tissue. Dancing lines echo the pattern of felled trees but also suggest that underlying life continues. I *have* seen in the landscape the colours I use, but I exaggerate them, make them more dramatic, bring them into collision with each other. I like using pure colour, without mixing it.'

She talks of getting herself psyched up for work in the studio, and her surfaces, with their urgent sweeps and Steadman-like splatterings, are alive with the excitement and energy of creative labour. There is no attempt to disguise her procedures or to feign completion. All too aware of humanity's frequently disastrous 'mastery' of nature, she refuses to submit the music of her complexly resonant landscapes to the impoverishing discipline of perspective. She can grow impatient with the rigidities of the rectangle, and explode her tableaux in irregular, tatty-edged shapes along the length of a wall. These apparent 'liberties' of form work in creative tension with carefully executed lines of stitching or gracefully delineated coils, dogsteeth, bones, human and animal figures. Art that purports to be simply representational or imagist offers to do most of the work for its spectators: what you see is what you get. Her paintings are not for the collector of 'framed views'. Mary Lloyd Jones wants to involve her audiences, to make them participators in, rather than merely consumers of, her landscapes. Is that long reddish line a distant road, a watercourse, the head of a hawk? What are we to make of these visitations from aboriginal or Beaker art that our 'educated' eyes are pleased to read as an 'N' or a 'Y' or a stylised breast? And if that ancient quotation really is a

Rough and Fragile Land

vagina with eyes, does that begin to undermine certain assumptions about the predominantly masculine nature of the language of art? We share in her playful sense of ambiguity, her delight in interconnections and the relatedness of forms.

It is only since 1989, when she gave up her job as visual arts officer for Dyfed, that Mary Lloyd Jones has been working as a full-time artist. Visits to America and Ireland, where she found cultures that value their artists, encouraged her to take that important step. 'In those two countries, if you're serious about your art, you do it full-time. You know that it's okay to do it, you are not a freak, it's not some kind of hole-in-the-corner activity. Everywhere is not like Wales or England'.

In Philadelphia her friend Kathy Quigley, who participated in the Wales/Philadelphia Visual Arts Exchange some years ago, works in a building which is five storeys high and has twenty artists' studios on each. 'Trucks were pulling into this building and paintings were going out: there was a market there. Lots of young professional people in America are buying art before they've bought their furniture.' It was frustrating to have to return to a country with an underdeveloped visual arts tradition, where few people visit art galleries and even fewer consider buying an original painting. 'There are now young Welsh artists, many of them women, who have gone to art school and want work in Wales. People should be buying this work and looking after these artists instead of concentrating solely on the mortgage and the Volvo. What we know about the earliest people, we know through art. And we are part of that continuity. If Wales can't be bothered about its art then it will disappear.'

The year 2001 finds Mary Lloyd Jones busier and more productive than ever. Travel – not only to Ireland and America, but Brittany, the Scottish Highlands and, in recent years, Rajasthan – has always refreshed her palate and proposed new ways of orchestrating colour. She manages, in spite of her foreign adventures and work for television and radio, to mount several exhibitions a year, and estimates that from the twelve or fifteen sketches that result from a day in the field she will produce annually about a hundred finished works.

Though rooted in *y fro Gymraeg*, Mary Lloyd Jones is neither land-locked nor fixed in history: the past for her, as for Iolo Morganwg, whose bardic alphabet inscribes shape-shifting messages across her landscapes, is an activist in the present. She is as intrigued by theories of relativity and chaos as by the desert light and sugared colours of a destination as new and strange to her as Rajasthan.

An exuberant celebrator of the diversity that feeds the very root of life, Mary Lloyd Jones invites us to enter into dialogue with the spirit of her chosen places, reconnecting our jaded, techno-conditioned sensibilities with those subterranean energies and '*Hen bethau anghofiedig dynol ryw*' (Old forgotten things of humankind), to quote Waldo Williams, which in our frenzied pursuit of novelty we ignore at our, and the planet's, peril.

LEAD MINES AND SCARS THE REMAINS OF WHAT WERE THE MOST IMPORTANT LEAD MINES IN BRITAIN CAN BE SEEN IN NORTH CEREDIGION, WHERE GENERATIONS OF MY FAMILY HAVE LIVED. MY WORK IS A RESPONSE TO THE HISTORY OF THE LAND WHICH CAN BE READ IN THE LEATS, SHAFTS, SPOIL TIPS AND RUINED BUILDINGS THAT CHARACTERISE THE LANDSCAPE AND PROVIDE A SENSE OF PLACE.

Cofio Mwyngloddio

Ystumtuen

Olion

Nant yr Arian

Scarred Hills

Red Kite

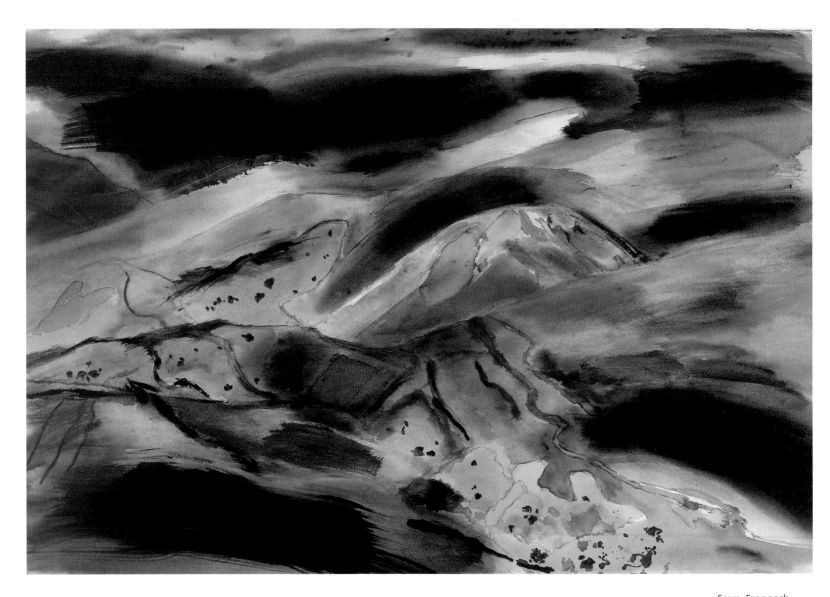

Scars, Frongoch

opposite Wounded Land

Pumlumon

Remembrancer *Mary Sara*

The serious contemporary artist who persists in painting, and whose roots lie in the experience of landscape, is sometimes regarded in certain quarters as a member of an endangered species worthy only of pity and protective charity. But even the most basic knowledge of the history of art indicates that great and lasting art is not about style or fashion but about sensibility. It is not, and never has been, just for depicting and naming, but for knowing and showing. Art is a vehicle for ideas, and for exploring significant events and experiences and the relationship of the personal to the universal: it should identify the universal in the particular. Above all art is, or should be, a means of communication of discoveries and propositions. In the presence of art of the quality and integrity of that of Mary Lloyd Jones it also becomes clear that the making of paintings can still be one of the most holistic and redemptive acts that the artist can perform in and for the society in which s/he lives.

Whether she is in her childhood landscape of the Rheidol Valley in the mountains of mid Wales, or in India, Brittany or Catalunya, Mary Lloyd Jones absorbs information with eye, brain, heart and hand. When we stand in the landscape, the shapes and angles, declivities and folds of the land and how they relate to each other not only provide the underlying mass and structure of what we see, but, like a blueprint or code, dictate the natural incidents of surface colours, patterns and textures as well as the man-made accidents of stainings, scars, plantings and interventions such as walls, spoil-heaps and roads. Initially, she seems to correspond to the notion of the artist propagated by Victorian writer and theorist John Ruskin as an individual who goes to nature 'in all singleness of heart and walks with her laboriously and trustingly, having no other thought but how best to penetrate her meaning'. Unfortunately, the stream of popular landscape painting that has flowed from some other (subsequently debased) Ruskinian ideas has been concerned only with representing scenery and views, but he also proposed, prophetically for his time, that the value of art was ultimately independent of representation. The great artists of the British landscape tradition, from Turner onwards, have all revealed things beyond appearances and demonstrated that landscape painting can be imaginative without being untrue. The Romantics went to nature for intimations of the sublime. For example, Caspar David Friedrich found the landscape drenched in symbolic allusions that rendered man insignificant and puny before the power of both nature and God, but the greatest value of Romanticism lies in the fact that, with its insistence on feeling and the artist's right to personal expression, it laid the foundation for a truly modern art. Though 'Romantic' is sometimes used as a term of abuse by post-modernists, the belief that the human imagination is inseparable from an empirical response to the natural, visible, world, continues to persist – and constantly re-invigorates not only contemporary art, but music and literature too. Conceptualism will prove to be a cul-de-sac up which its proponents will disappear, and abstraction is only occasionally now saved from sterility by a handful of artists with secret Romantic attachments in their souls. The notion at the heart of Romanticism that art and nature together can offer a redemptive experience will endure in some form or another until the next millennium. It is after all merely the most recent flowering of the cult of nature that lies at the roots of western European culture.

Even the most thoroughly urbanised people in a post-industrial society increasingly dominated by technocracy recognise an atavistic connection with the land. They know that engagement with landscape engages the spirit, and respond instinctively and hungrily to the work of sculptors such as Andy Goldsworthy, Peter Randall Page, and David Nash, who work with natural materials in highly individual ways. Their respectful, not to say loving, handling of ice, stone or wood to disclose aspects of our dependent relationship to the land that supports all life strikes a chord which resonates far beyond the cognoscenti of the art world. Like Goldsworthy *et al.*, Mary Lloyd Jones fears that our relationship with the land is in danger of becoming only skin-deep, that we can no longer read what it has to tell us in the way that earlier peoples could. She attends to the landscape with intelligence, with a deep awareness and knowledge of its history, bringing all that she is to the empirically observed facts in front of her. Due to this intense engagement, her first studies crackle with energy and excitement. With a kind of speed-writing, sometimes in graphite smudges and scribbles, more often in colour and marks, she dashes down her first response, simplifying the essentials and recording a selection from what she sees to create a personal precis of an experience of a time and place. These small, fast, paintings contain what she calls 'direct quotations of colours and significant configurations' but they are evocative *aide-mémoires* rather than literal records. Even so, the artist's eye has made particular choices; the formal decisions of what to put where, next to what and how, which govern the creative act, are already operating in that immediate selection. All the source material which is orchestrated into, and gives structure to, the large oil paintings in which she creates another landscape in paint is in the studies, but, because art is not dependent on external reality, what happens next comes from who she is.

The Welsh painter, engraver and writer David Jones wrote: 'In our present megalopolitan technocracy the artist must still be a rememberer (part of the official bardic function in earlier phases of society) – a shower forth of things'. It is an ancient role which began with the member of the tribe who lifted his or her eyes from the task of survival and said Look! or asked Why? How? What if? – then shaped with their hands or said, or sang, a celebration or proposed an answer. They survived because the tribe valued the role; they flourished in full view, part of the everyday. Today, in an excruciatingly complex society, artists are largely alienated from their public, making their work in private places, but the writer about art is privileged to be able to scrutinise the process and is given the opportunity to interpret the information so gathered for the lay audience. Besides the practical paraphernalia of materials, the contents of Mary Lloyd Jones's studio are evidence of the concerns and interests that motivate her and clues to her interior life. The books that lie on tables and shelves are indications of a micro-culture or a one-person soul library. They nourish ideas, expand knowledge and confirm that as a solitary artist in a particular culture she is part of a timeless, seamless genealogy of rememberers and makers. Books on 3,000 years of megalithic culture, rock art and petroglyphs are stacked near Marija Gimbutas' huge volumes on fifth- and sixth-century BC cultures, in which sacred scripts like

Iaith Cofio

runes record a culture of the Goddess.[1] They tower over slim copies of Iolo Morganwg's *Coelbren y Beirdd* (Bardic Alphabet) and there is a scattering of books on Indian decorative patterns, and quilts. These are some of the rich variety of sources with which Mary Lloyd Jones identifies and which she affirms as collaborators across the millennia, not forgetting the grandmother who stitched her innate creativity into a quilt, not knowing that she was an artist, and Lewis Morris who penned his extraordinary technical records of the Cardiganshire Mines in 1742.[2]

This brings us to a consideration of the most obviously abstract element of painting – the mark, and in the case of Mary Lloyd Jones, the symbol abstracted from nature and knowledge. Morris's curious marks, hatchings and symbols convey on paper the information he gathered on the ground, and he used multiple perspectives in a single sheet. There were no rules for what he was trying to do so he mapped his discoveries by any means at his disposal – or he invented new means – as does Mary Lloyd Jones. Even the uninitiated can conjecture that pre-literate signs and symbols could have developed alongside verbal and written vocabularies, that a visual language may in fact have been a more universally intelligible means of communicating concepts and ideas within and between societies than spoken or written words. Conversely, symbols and secret languages have also been used to keep esoteric knowledge the preserve of the initiated few, but in the main the purpose had been more generously exoteric: literature and art came into being because every society has known that what is worth remembering or knowing has to be fixed and shared if the culture of that society is to survive. The importance of language to a people cannot be underestimated and it should be better understood by the rest of the inhabitants of the British Isles that the existence and survival of the Welsh language are part of their history too. As a Welsh-speaking artist Mary Lloyd Jones is working in a culture whose strongest aspect is a literature in which there is a colourful, playful use of language in poems, myths and histories.

The Welsh imagination revelled in 'magic realism' centuries before that phrase was popularly associated with the work of recent South American novelists. A strong narrative in which the quotidian real co-exists with the magically unreal is characterised also by a sense of recurrence, displacement, and of fractured time. When she paints, Mary Lloyd Jones is working with time and place. The time she stood and drew a hillside. The time in the studio. The time when livid stains were produced as men took silver, lead and copper from the rock and left the hillsides ravaged and an oppressed people in pain. The time when people carved spirals on rocks, when they made sheep folds, when they stitched their creativity into quilts. The time in India when she experienced the most visual culture she had ever been in, where everyone is an artist with colour and pattern and she was dazzled by colours of apricot, peach, orange and brilliant sky blues inside and outside their houses. The time when lines were cut into the peat and then became glyphs written in paint on canvas; when the words Iaith and Cofio (language and memory) in the bardic alphabet entered a painting and gave it a quality of epic potentiality. As with the multiple perspectives she uses, often within a single painting, sometimes flying over, sometimes across from, sometimes it seems from within the landscape, it could be dizzying except for the fact that she is in control. Her life is in her art and she knows where she is going.

It is neither possible nor useful to make a distinction between the painter and the thinker, between the instinctive and intellectual. As we have seen, the needs of a painting – for marks that enliven or make the strands of a narrative cohere – are met from a store of knowledge, but it is the painting not the ideas that dictate what is chosen and where it is placed. When, like David Bomberg, she strives to express 'the spirit in the mass' and to acknowledge respectfully the independent life of the landscape, instinct and practice conjoin on the surface of the canvas as she places colours and forms, and turns observed phenomena into symbols capable of carrying an impressive freight of ideas. But above all, I would suggest that, as a painter, her most powerful and personal language is colour. Colour is to art what sound is to music, and it is colour in her work that reveals that which is beyond appearances, colour which articulates those otherwise inexpressible feelings for which language is inadequate but to express which she became a painter. A composer could write the equivalent of her paintings with dark-toned bass chords or throbbing drums like the reverberative passages of deep, dark colours; strings, arias or cymbals for the high-pitched colours and voices singing the symbols and word fragments. It is a good test of a painter's truth if, after a day with the work, you go out into the world and see it through their eyes. It has happened to me countless times with Turner, especially after immersion in the northern landscapes I know so well. Emerging from the Tate Gallery onto a navy-blue lamplight embankment after seeing Whistler's evocations of the same place was magical. Peter Lanyon gives me back my experience of Cornwall, Paul Nash that of beech hangers in Oxfordshire, Winifred Nicholson that of rain-soaked Cumbrian fells, Joan Eardley that of the Aberdeenshire coast, and in mid Wales, driving through rain and sun I was in Mary Lloyd Jones's translucent watercolours and glancing up to mountainsides which were her canvases brushed with intense oil colours of drenched pastures, blue distances, orange bracken and dark, glistening rocks.

Paradoxically, when she began her painting life she says that she had to forget her Welshness. At the time, being from a Welsh peasant background was considered to be a huge disadvantage; it had implications of a damaged culture whose people had had to deny their inheritance in order to succeed on the oppressor's terms. Literature and music were the ascendant media because they preserved and furthered the linguistic heritage but visual art, because it was identified with the alien, English culture, was less valued. Though the Welsh landscape had been picked over, celebrated even, Welshness had simply not been a subject for visual art and it was some time before she was ready, empowered by maturity and skill, to give expression to her sense of personal identity. The artist is always the outsider and the female Welsh artist is no stranger to the feelings of frustration engendered by invisible barriers constructed and maintained by others. However, if there is one vitally distinctive and positive quality possessed by female artists it is that they are both able and willing to transform confrontation into communication. Our damaged and threatened environment, the result of greed and short-termism, is in great need of such affirmative action. The passion for her homeland is there for us to see in her paintings, but Mary Lloyd Jones's creativity is not limited by geography and history; she is fully aware that the microcosm she examines and celebrates can stand not only for other cultures both known to her and unknown, but also for the whole planet. As Alfred de Musset wrote: 'Great artists have no country'.

Art at this level demands that the contents of the unconscious as well as the imagination have to find concrete form, with no self-protective editing, and it can be a lonely and risky business. Artists are used to this, and to their marginalisation within society, but it does not make it an easy life to choose. But if, since the Renaissance at least, the artist has always been the outsider, the regional artist today can be perceived as doubly so in the metro-centred art-universe which its doyens, who think they write the rules and who certainly wield an inordinate amount of power, regard as the only place to be. Even more of a problem has been that 'regional' has become synonymous with 'provincial', which has historically been a pejorative critical term implying a parochial lack of originality or sophistication. While distance, either geographical or intellectual, from the perceived centre can lead to isolation from the flow of ideas, lack of stimulus and crippling introversion, it can also confer independence and freedom from the sterility of a monoculture and therefore potentially provide a rich soil in which to grow. This is certainly the case with Mary Lloyd Jones, chiefly because her pride in her nationality has not prevented her from seeking cross-cultural and international influences and stimuli. Unfortunately, when the metro-centred culture is also that of the alien 'other', then the Welsh artist, who rightly wishes to see their work valued and evaluated in the widest possible context, can find themselves in a double-bind. By adopting a positive pride in the ability to engage in a confident and mutually beneficial exchange between equals rather than adopting a defensive position, Mary Lloyd Jones has triumphantly bypassed one of the curses of the so-called regional artist. Taking a wider view, with the dissolution of the notion of 'the other' as the scapegoat for failure or inadequacy is also removed, which is why artists of the calibre of Mary Lloyd Jones must first be celebrated in their own country. By cherishing home-grown excellence, the rest of the society, and its artists, can be empowered to develop their maximum potential, unfettered by the past. Mary Lloyd Jones is now being honoured in her own country at an age when she is 'too young for people to believe that the most ambitious work has necessarily been accomplished'.[3]

Ambition takes many forms. The artist needs what she calls 'space in the head', uninterrupted time and the possibility of exhibiting the work – especially the works on a larger scale – in spaces where her expansive ideas will be

38

able to breathe and have maximum impact. By virtue of the ambitions she has always had for her art, and in the context of painting in Britain and Europe, it is appropriate to describe her as a Welsh artist of international standing. Ambition for Mary Lloyd Jones has nothing to do with fame and fortune but everything to do with communicating urgent messages about the state of our world today through the facture of painting – messages about power and powerlessness, history and timelessness, pain and the transformative power of the imagination. Although keenly conscious of the past she is a poet, in paint, of her own time, one of Shelley's 'unacknowledged legislators'.

Since the invention of photography, painting has been pronounced dead many times, but nobody told the corpse. Those who misdiagnosed the condition of painting were the same people who misunderstood its particular nature and, I believe, fundamentally missed the point about what art is for and what artists are about. If one's only source of information and experience of contemporary art were the weightiest art magazines, television coverage of the Turner prize, the collecting habits of a handful of wealthy media moguls and the bizarre behaviour of a small coterie of youngish artists as related via the popular press, then one could well imagine that every medium but paint was in use at the turn of the millennium. The impression of art gained from the most raucously vocal sources would be that artists have become mere reporters of the ugliness of urban life and the worst aspects of human nature, that they have become purveyors of sensation and, whatever the subject, have abrogated responsibility for any kind of useful transformation of experience. It would also appear that some have abandoned the attempt to find the common ground with their audience from which a dialogue is possible. The negativity inherent in much contemporary art is perhaps unsurprising but it too often offers judgements without analysis and displays symptoms of the ills of society without

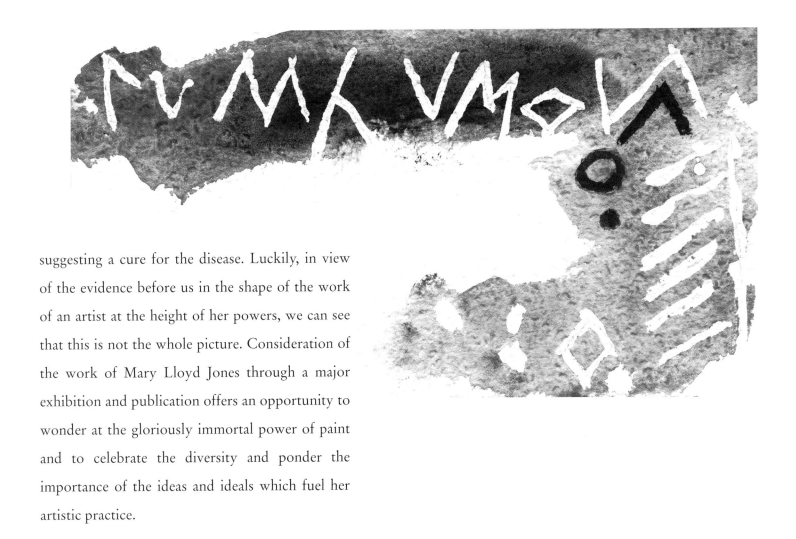

suggesting a cure for the disease. Luckily, in view of the evidence before us in the shape of the work of an artist at the height of her powers, we can see that this is not the whole picture. Consideration of the work of Mary Lloyd Jones through a major exhibition and publication offers an opportunity to wonder at the gloriously immortal power of paint and to celebrate the diversity and ponder the importance of the ideas and ideals which fuel her artistic practice.

[1] Marija Gimbutas, *The Language of the Goddess* (Thames and Hudson, 1989).
[2] David Bick and Philip Wyn Davies, *Lewis Morris and the Cardiganshire Leadmines* (National Library of Wales, 1994).
[1] Menna Elfyn, *Trying the Line: A Volume of Tribute to Gillian Clarke* (Gomer Press, 1997).

opposite Jaipur III

TRAVELS IN INDIA

MY AIM IN VISITING INDIA WAS TO IMMERSE MYSELF IN A CULTURE WHERE THE USE OF COLOUR IS FLUENT, SPONTANEOUS AND SOPHISTICATED. CRAFTSMANSHIP SURVIVES IN SPITE OF WESTERN INFLUENCES AND CAN BE ENJOYED IN THE PATTERN-MAKING AND EMBELLISHMENT SEEN ON ALL SURFACES.

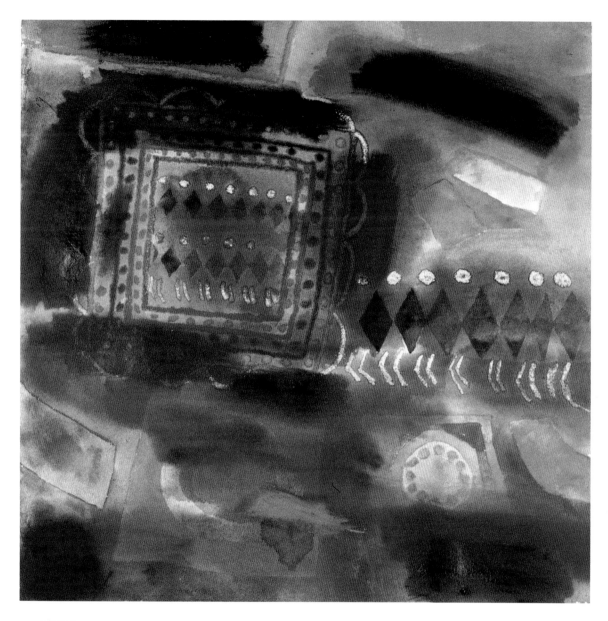

Jaipur II

opposite India

Jaisalmer II

opposite Udaipur

Kishanpol Bazaar

Jaipur I

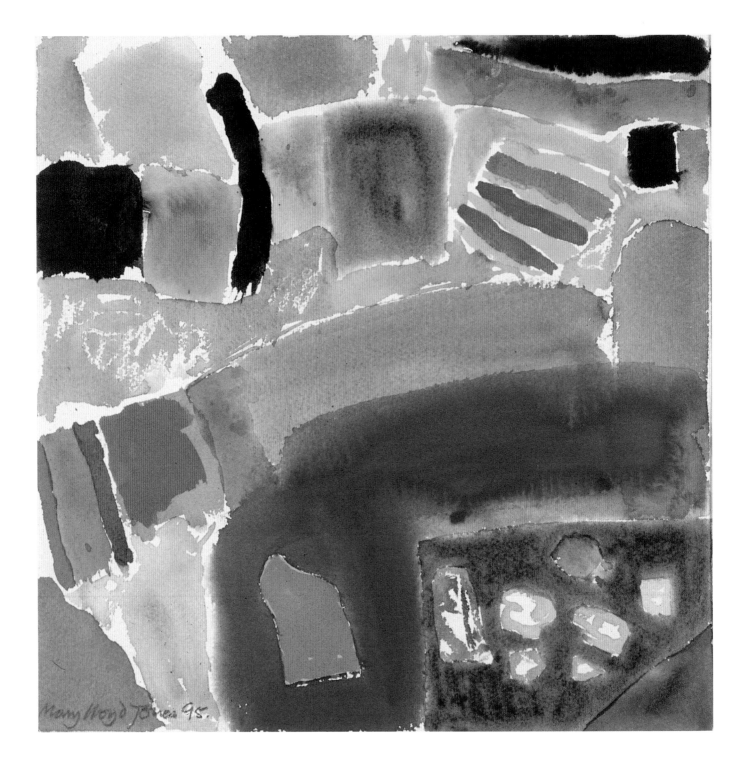

Mary Lloyd Jones 95.

Jaisalmer I

opposite Mandawa

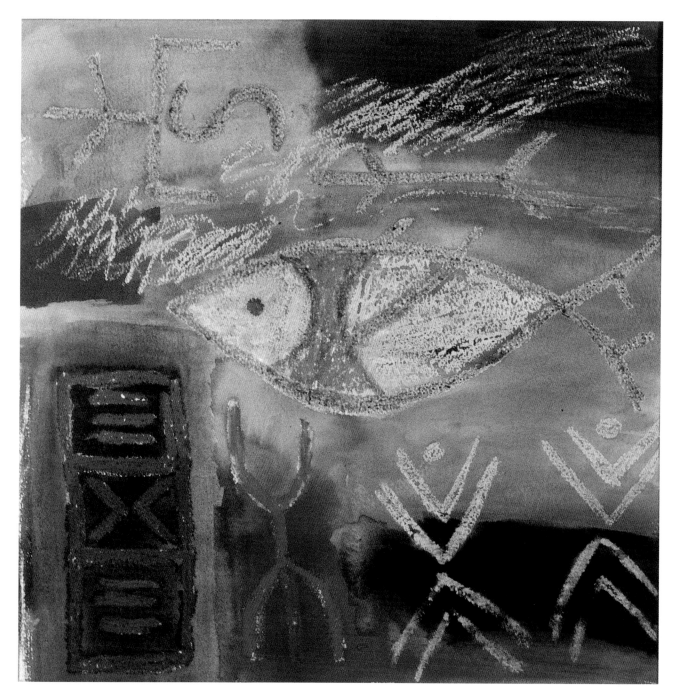

Bagru Fish

Cloth Fields

Yellow Cloth

Kite Festival

First Language *Derek Hyatt*

'TO KNOW THE FUTURE, STUDY THE PAST' *Japanese Proverb*

Nature and man have continually re-shaped Wales. On any walk through her landscape today we come across traces of the past, events happening now and clues to the future. As Wales re-shapes herself once again she needs artists of vision and imagination.

West Wales is particularly rich in history, myth and legend. Modern artists working in this landscape must decide whether they wish to accept, deny or celebrate these connections with the past. The works of Mary Lloyd Jones are a celebration of the west Wales landscape, its history and its prehistory. Her images show her exploring different approaches to making modern landscape art. Mary works towards an art capable of responding to the wide range of references and experiences available to artists in the twenty-first century.

To some people 'landscape painting' is concerned with descriptive imitation of views and objects. Mary's vision is of nature as energy, movement, delight and mystery. Her work combines the discoveries in colour made by modern art and psychology with the graphic language and magic substances of prehistoric art. This is experimental art by a mature artist.

Mary works fast and takes risks; the results look urgent. 'My paintings must surprise me,' she has said. Cloud shadows on the move, sudden rainbows, colours on the move. Shapes with no name. Forms in and out of focus. Bracken, earth, water, sky, crag, sunset. New images of places she has known all her life. Innocence and experience asking each other questions.

Much of Mary's childhood was spent alone, exploring the waterfalls, rockpools and cascades of Devil's Bridge, near Aberystwyth. Over many years the Rheidol Valley has provided a rich seam of images. Like a prospector or miner, she has 'worked the valley'. Some paintings show the multicoloured lead and silver spills. Several paintings have been triggered by a ghostly mineral spoil, known locally as 'The Stag'. The antlers are eroding but the complete image stays in the memory. An accidental scar of industrial waste becomes a kind of prehistoric emblem. As if an unknown ritual left a trace for us to interpret. For a moment that sign is out of time, floating in our mind's eye. Very strange and provocative. Now or then? Would a North American Indian or Bushman hunter shoot an arrow across the valley to honour this image? Ask a child of eight. Children still inhabit such landscapes of the imagination.

Mary has spent a lifetime teaching at all levels of art education in this country. Out of this experience has evolved her conviction that art must surprise, delight and yet touch deep chords within us. Her own art is experimental; we see, for example, the risks she takes with colour. Where does the need to put dark orange against pale pink come from? Where does that lilac against that yellow take us? Colour as a language.

Some years ago Mary found, in a drawer, an old patchwork quilt made by her great-grandmother. This was a revelation, for it showed her in a moment that a member of her own family years ago had made a large abstract colour piece; loaded with family history and association, simple in form, complicated in colour. How marvellous, she thought, to find evidence of a woman artist making such positive art, using colour in such a dramatic, large-scale, public and emotional way. Here for Mary was permission, shock, challenge and delight all at once.

The great colourists of the Modern Movement, Kandinsky, Matisse and Klee, all fled their own folk art memories of Russia, Africa and Central Europe. Gradually colour took over their art as the main ingredient. Klee wrote in his African diary: 'Colour and I am one'. These great explorers of modern art were also touched by the expressive forms of primitive art. They noticed that tribal art across the world strove to simplify ideas and concepts into stark shapes and signs: a visual language appropriate to song, dance and ritual, in media and scale appropriate to hilltop, beach and cave.

Some years ago Mary visited Rombalds Moor above Ilkley in Yorkshire. This moor is one of the richest locations of Bronze Age rock art in Europe. Local archaeologists have recorded over three hundred carved rocks there. These carvings include shallow cups and rings, rows of dots, lines and curves, enclosures and loops, and in one case a spinning swastika emblem. Many interpretations of these signs are possible. They are clearly an abstract language of thought. A recent book by the American Marija Gimbutas entitled *The Language of the Goddess* brings together the full European story of such art.[1] This is a thrilling book. To realise that, right across Europe in Bronze Age times, in each village, local craftsmen and artists were working and inventing in such a sophisticated abstract visual language, is chastening. We have much to learn from our 'primitive' ancestors.

Mary's paintings include primitive signs dancing through her landscapes. She is testing whether such shapes and lines still contain meanings for us. Archaeologists are now more open to the idea that simple signs can have multiple meanings and that is their strength and mystery today. You will see from drawings first made by Mary out on the moor at Ilkley, that at first the carved sign lies on the rock. The circle lies down in perspective at our feet. In the later versions, the circle and signs dance in midair, before our eyes, like a projection from memory. This break from perspective space to floating space moves Mary's landscapes into new dimensions.

Perspective becomes obsolete for Pembrokeshire's windswept hillsides, cloudscapes and folded volcanic cliffs. Outdoor experience demands other concepts of space and time. Above Carningli the hunting buzzard searches the hillsides. The artist's eye searches those same hillsides for colours, shapes and signs. In the landscapes of Mary Lloyd Jones we float, feel the buoyancy of flight and make sudden diagonal swoops of discovery. Ecology, Geology, Chaos Theory, The Uncertainty Principle, Local Folklore and 'Once upon a Time' are all different viewpoints. All different ways of entering the landscape and finding new pathways to understanding.

Look at the great Celtic cross in Nevern churchyard. Each carved compartment contains a map to infinity and an invitation to dream. The stone stands for a whole tradition of imagination and belief. What did we lose when we invented words?

Landmarks

Bro

Artists such as Mary Lloyd Jones show us nature as a metaphor for change. Outdoor colour and light do us good. Movement through space is a tonic. We feel more alive outdoors. More able to be positive about the future. As a society our attitudes to nature must change. As Wilfred Owen wrote: 'All the poet can do is warn'.

Looking is a skill. We search for meanings and objects we recognise. Shapes and colours remind us of memories in our own life. Certain lines and movements remind us of places outdoors and the feelings we had in these spaces. On clifftops and hillsides the way space opens and closes can be most affecting. Cloud and rock shapes can lead us towards mystical experiences of awe and wonder or just remind us of childhood picnics when all the world was new and unexplored.

Let's explore a stream of associations initiated for the individual spectator by a Mary Lloyd Jones painting. First of all we experience an all-over side-to-side immersion in colour and movement. Blue shapes move and blur their edges over pink washes. No objects here to name, just the feeling of being in outdoor space. Some movements are complete, some are cut off by the edge. We re-live the brush making blue move in this way. We follow the trace across the paper, the now of it happening. If in our mind we now flick to landscape memories the blue becomes mass or space and could become an afternoon in Pembrokeshire walking near St David's Head, the first day on holiday, a great feeling of release and space. Looking is a skill. Remembering is a skill. Painting is translating, remembering into colour, giving structure to fleeting feelings. Painting is the skill of shaping feelings so the artist works with hand and eye, colours and edges to re-create moments out of doors when the landscape said to the artist, 'Stop your ordinary life. Grasp the image now. Look now. Something out there in the juxtapositions of nature set off a circuit of connections in the artist's mind. Try and hold that group of forms before they change and fade. This is the Skill. To see feelings and catch them in midair.' In the completed painting we experience a sequence of darks over light, of coolness broken by walls, of warm bracken zigzags drawn fast over yellow. Does this Dance convince us of a Truth? Do we mind if Darks threaten Rain, is our body triggered for change? Raindrops on the windscreen? The yellow shape is yellow, then becomes a sunlit field and then back to yellow as we move off onto a cold grey shadow. Is a shadow as real as the

Cwm Rheidol

opposite Study 1

object? Outdoors each dark has reflected light and colour. All light outdoors moves and changes. Our light-metre eyes tell us. The red dot on the camera warns us. The landscape artist's eye/mind/heart/ has to say YES faster than the camera. Faster than one tenth at F/16 YES – and we all have this skill, which is why we have our eyes backed up by the incredible circuits of the mind. As Darwin said, 'The eye still scares me.' Leonardo saw the world with his mind and used his eye as a knife. This is the skill of art.

Mary Lloyd Jones risks working from nature. Nature is always too much. Always changing. Some artists settle for picture-making to formulae. They have a vocabulary of art-moves that worked in the past so why risk the disappointments, tensions and emotions of real life? Theirs is the publicly recognisable style – no sudden changes of mood and intensity. But nature is always changing her mind. The ice pool suddenly gives way underfoot. The cumulous cloud looks static until we draw it, then unseen, its shape has changed. All nature moves at different speeds. 'Very queer,' says Ted Hughes's Wodwo, but he goes on looking, turning over the leaves by the river bank, finding that the underside of a brown green grey is suddenly flesh-pink vivid.

'I can't draw,' says the student 'and it takes too long anyway.' (Goes back into a darkened room, switches on the screen, presses buttons. Discovers his or her memory bank is empty so rearranges other people's answers until teabreak.)

Meanwhile, outdoors on the hill, the urgent cloud shadows cross the colour-drenched landscape. Mary Lloyd Jones again takes risks to discover old truths. We are fallible, we imagine and feel. We desire that nature takes us back. The cloudbank opens up and light floods the valley. The artist's hand responds. Painting is fast and slow. And very human. Every hesitation shows. Moments of truth appear as if by magic.

Later we walk the hills seeing them through artists' eyes. After rain the clarity of space and colour is good for the soul. How could we forget?

[1] Marija Gimbutas, *The Language of the Goddess* (Thames and Hudson, 1989).

MARKS AND ALPHABETS

PREHISTORIC CUP AND RING MARKS ON ILKLEY MOOR LED ME TO AN INTEREST IN EARLY ALPHABETS. 'OGHAM' IS AN ANCIENT ALPHABET USED BY THE BARDS OF BRITAIN AND IRELAND AS A MEANS OF PASSING CODED MESSAGES.

Discovery of Ancient Signs

In the National Library of Wales, I found in the material on Iolo Morganwg fascinating details of his bardic alphabet, 'Coelbren'. Iolo Morganwg was a renowned eighteenth-century Welsh scholar, poet, antiquarian and stonemason.

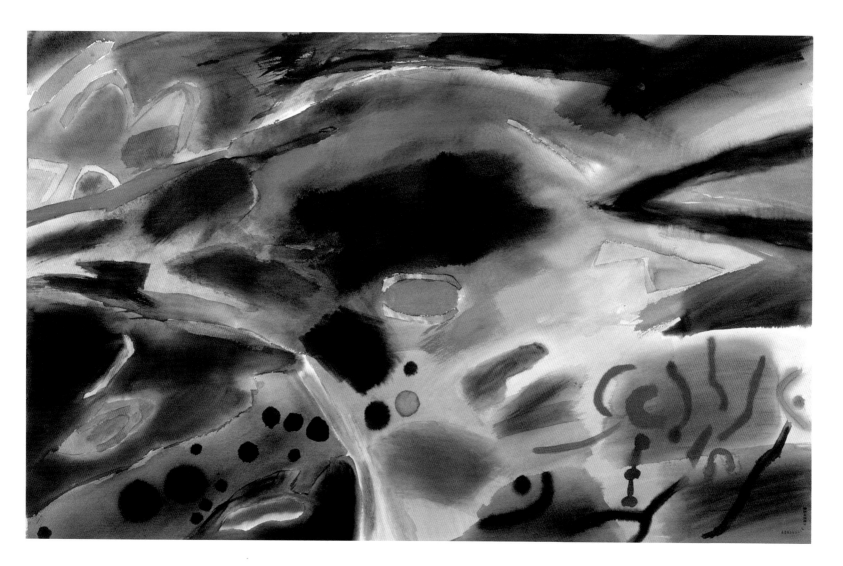

Song Lines

66   Barclodiad y Gawres II

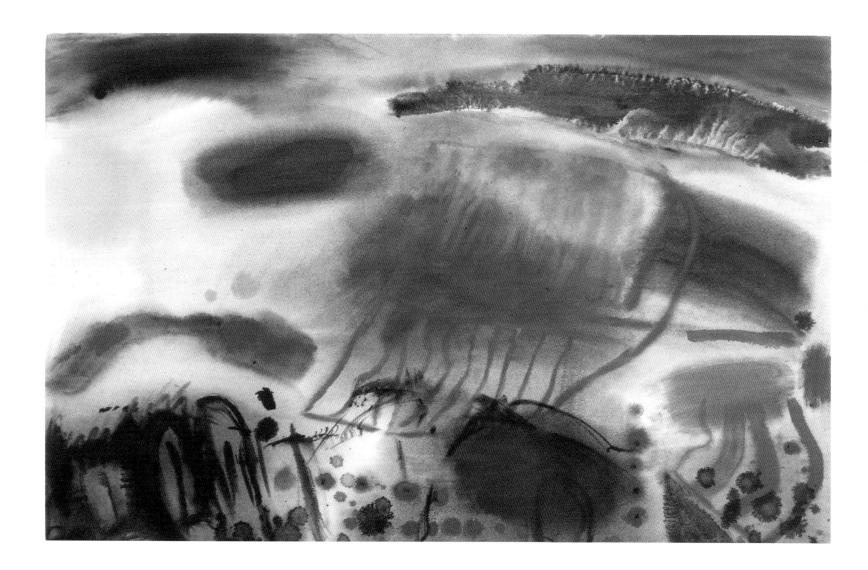

Arad Goch

Heniaith

opposite Gaia

Pwy Fedr Ddarllen y Ddaear (Waldo Williams)

opposite Wild Sound

Copa Pumlumon

opposite Barclodiad y Gawres III

Study 2

An Encompassing Vision   *Peter Abbs*

We are in an unprecedented crisis in the history of the visual arts. It is a crisis of representation and meaning. The case against the various avant-gardes of the last century can now be presented with a philosophical cogency which has still to be recognised. Quite simply, the visual arts have too often failed to represent and aesthetically embody the full range and the peculiar depth of the human spirit. They have failed to connect with the historic past. And they have failed to find an audience beyond a tiny, faddish, media-centred minority. Instead of addressing and liberating the imagination much modern and contemporary art has merely added to the symptoms of decay, loss and futility. As we begin the third millennium we are in need of a more fundamental imaginative orientation and a deep historical, spiritual and ecological re-connection. In the work of Mary Lloyd Jones we encounter an art which is struggling to create such an encompassing vision.

Mary Lloyd Jones works in Aberbanc, in the heart of rural Wales. She settled there in 1976, turning a traditional primary school into a vast studio area. Here she works with a single-minded tenacity committed not only to her own evolving work but also to the regeneration of art in Wales. Her background is Welsh and Welsh-speaking; it is also deeply rural.

Being an artist in any place is not easy, being an artist in Wales seemed at that time to be a contradiction in terms, a stark oxymoron. For it would seem that the expressive energies of the Welsh culture, for a complex variety of reasons, rushed almost entirely into the language of poetry and rhetoric leaving the other arts, especially the visual, neglected and misunderstood. For a number of years Mary Lloyd Jones clearly suffered a sense of isolation, an acute feeling of exile in her own culture. How could one become a painter in Wales where there was no sustained visual arts tradition?

Of course, like earlier Romantics, one could turn for inspiration to the great and ancient mountains of Wales, but Mary Lloyd Jones discovered something else, something more intimate, something much closer to home. She was given a quilt made by her great-grandmother. Here was a visual artefact made by her own class, her own people, her own family. It was clearly functional but it was also clearly beautiful. One had only to lift it off the bed and hang it on the wall to grasp the compelling symmetry of its form. It was, at the same moment, art and craft. It was both public and intimate – belonging, as it did, to the obvious daily needs of a living culture. For the artist it was a revelation.

The quilt proclaims three things. *Art belongs here where we live and work. It is committed to beauty. It can be made by women.*

In the 1970s Mary Lloyd Jones consciously sought to extend the tradition that was historically hers. She engaged with fabrics and with the labour traditionally associated with women – with washing, sewing, dyeing. But the themes of her work expanded to embrace the drama of natural landscape, the magical markings of ancestors and the power of ancient cave paintings. Her paintings show recognisable landscapes indelibly marked by the struggles and aspirations of human consciousness. The quilt-tradition was being acknowledged, extended and transformed. Its influence can be detected, if more indirectly, in the paintings, particularly the watercolours. Here some of the standard geometrical figures of the quilt composition can be witnessed (but with new spiritual resonances in play) as also the clear patches of colour placed adroitly side by side to make the pattern of the picture. As an artist friend said to me about one of Mary's landscapes: 'It is as if you could pull the painting over your head and sleep under it.'

But Mary Lloyd Jones's work also belongs unequivocally to a central European movement which we could term *Spiritual Expressionism*. It is a strong gestural tradition in the visual arts where the final vision of the painting is discovered in the engaged physical handling of the very stuff of paint. In this school much of the painter's meaning is apprehended in the startingly fresh textures and transformations of the labile material – simply, paint in all its volatility – as it is applied to the canvas or paper. In this tradition one would have to place Rembrandt, who adored the moist, shining, palpable *substance* of paint – but also the twentieth-century painters Nolde, Bomberg and Hitchens.

At its most radical this tradition creates a kind of symphonic painting where the colours and tones, working simultaneously, create a powerful mood through which the meaning of the spirit is articulated and the ineffable given sudden unexpected accommodation. Bomberg talked famously of 'the spirit in the mass'. The analogue is with music – though unlike music the marks still often retain a reference to a recognisable physical world which they seek to interpret – and the method that of the most urgent intuition. Tellingly, these painters have exerted a seminal influence on the work of Mary Lloyd Jones.

She invariably works with great rapidity, allowing her spontaneous quick-moving intuitions to determine the urgent flow of paint and to resolve its unexpected meetings and chance collisions at top speed. *Carpe Diem!* At best, the result is a painting which has an irrepressible freshness – rather like the perception of God on the first day of Creation. Often, looking at her work we feel we are looking down from a great height. We see an aerial view as suddenly glimpsed by a divine bird. Perspective (that tedious art of calculation) yields here to simultaneous vision and the experience of Paradise – for we are not looking *at* but rather participating *in* what we see. All is immediate flow. The landscape a river of colour.

Much of Mary's work is celebratory and exerts an instant magic. And yet it is not always as unambiguous as that – for many of the Welsh landscapes depict the Rheidol Valley with its ground scarred by the disused lead mines and disfigured by the colonial angular planting of countless conifers. In some of these fine paintings a savage anger dismembers the natural forms and an inchoate rage splatters the canvas. And yet, even so, there are points of redemption. For example, in some of the turbulent Rheidol Valley paintings, an ancient mystical language will be subtly introduced or intimated, or a divine geometry – often, the sacred triangle – will emerge to complement the turbulent flux. The unnatural wounds of the landscape, the deep industrial scars, the old derelict castles are there, but even as they appear they suggest something infinitely more, an even older order that lies beyond them and before them. For the paintings are deeply polysemous and, unlike the pessimistic poetry of R.S. Thomas, fundamentally affirmative of life, at least when it is lived in a connected web of relationships – ecological, human and sacred.

Barclodiad y Gawres I

Coed

Felled Trees, Ystumtuen

opposite Clwtwaith

This brings me to the third great force working in and through the paintings. The more one considers and contemplates the work, the more one becomes aware of a spiritual visual language. Her landscape is not 'an environment' – that ugly word showing our mechanical distance from Nature – but more like a shrine of the Goddess. One of her works is actually called *Barclodiad Y Gawres* [The Goddess with an Apronful]. The many marks that congregate at unexpected points in the landscapes are neither doodles nor the arbitrary deposits of idle fantasy, but the dramatic marks of the missing Goddess, her ancient signs and signatures. The zigzag lines, the serpentine curves, the spiralling shapes, the dark triangles – all invoke the absence of the female God. This is Her old visual language and slowly it begins to address our impoverished souls. The lines are not casual, for they repeat and extend the very marks made in Palaeolithic and Neolithic times on rocks and stones and tombs, in the open air as, also, in the darkness of the caves. These markings, which compose an iconography in their own right, have been collected and interpreted in Marija Gimbutas' great book *The Language of the Goddess* – a book which has inspired Mary Lloyd Jones and been a formative influence on her late work.[1]

The conscious resuscitation of the bardic alphabet of Iolo Morganwg and the ancient Irish Ogham serves a similar purpose. The bold geometrical words move like dark presences across some of the landscapes as if to reclaim an earlier and broken contract – a contract which the painter wishes to honour again, a contract where the word and the world corresponded and were as one. Here the aim of the painting is to re-assert for modern times a lost connection, at once sacred and ecological. This, surely, is a clear and courageous answer to the exhausted avant gardes of the metropolis. *Connect. Connect the Earth to the missing Goddess. And connect both to the eternal imagination.*

No artist works alone – and if she did, then no one would understand her. The artist always stands inside history and culture. There is no alternative. But the aim is not merely to reflect or repeat what has been created by others. Far from it. The aim is dialectical engagement and cultural transformation in our own time, in our own place, in our own idiom. At best, this inward revision creates further common vision, a compelling sense of meaning and possibility. At first, this is experienced as a sense of startled recognition, a quiver of intellectual joy, a spiritual *yes*. A fuller

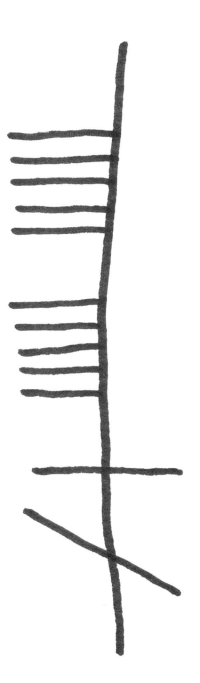

understanding comes gradually in its wake. This is the case with nearly all forms of aesthetic appreciation.

The great poet-philosopher, Nietzsche, wrote in *The Will To Power*: 'What does a pessimistic art signify? Is it not a *contradicio*? – Yes.' The late twentieth century after the first high period of Modernism was marked not only by pessimistic art, but by an art which delighted in its own much vaunted vacuity. The notion of the signifier without the signified has become a tedious cliché. It is time to show the vivid reciprocal relationship between art and life again and to affirm the power of the imagination. Mary Lloyd Jones's work marks a way forward. She has discovered the elements of an encompassing understanding and a powerful way of representing it. We should watch her sure development and be ready to learn.

[1] Marija Gimbutas, *The Language of the Goddess* (Thames and Hudson, 1989).

opposite Sussex Fields

OTHER PLACES TRAVELLING INVARIABLY GIVES AN ARTIST NEW IDEAS, AND INFLUENCES SUBSEQUENT WORK. BUT WHAT IS ALSO INTERESTING IS THAT ON RETURNING HOME, ONE CAN SEE FAMILIAR PLACES WITH NEW EYES AND A FRESH PERSPECTIVE.

Rhaeadr Nant Gwrtheyrn

opposite Plage de Guillien

Nant Gwrtheyrn

Carn Menyn

'Granite from Anglesey. Is it this/we tread on, this starry pavement,/a glittering milky way underfoot?'

from 'Earth Story' by Gillian Clarke

Parys Mountain

Farrera, Catalunya

Dyffryn Nantlle

Knock-na-rea

Highland Sky

The Lit Bush   *Gillian Clarke*

Driving home from an exhibition of Mary Lloyd Jones's work, I saw a vision. The A487 dissolved and I drove straight through the painter's lens into another country. All around me lay the hills of Ceredigion, lapped and folded in a net of fields scattered with farms. I thought I knew it, a place where a declining agriculture is once more changing an ancient and beautiful landscape. Hedges are destroyed. New wire and post fences appear. Stone farmhouses and barns collapse. Concrete bungalows and vast sheds rise in their place. Black polythene parcels of silage are piled in the fields, polythene rags flap in the hedgerows. Close to the road a quarry face reads 'Cofiwch Dryweryn'. A third generation of anonymous patriots refreshes the graffiti every now and again, so that the message seems as new as when my father first told me of the valley drowned by a reservoir to provide water for a distant city.

What the windscreen frames is transformed. The rock is a slab of paint applied with a palette knife. The landscape re-shapes to a pattern of stone-slippages, purples, gold, slate lozenges, the glaciers' calligraphy. All those translucencies, slabs, washes and abstract scratchings of colour are fresh from the gallery, familiar but translated into another language. Two landscapes lie about me, one over the other, paint and soil, both mine, the scarred and broken place of ancestry, of alienation and belonging.

I am forced to look again and to extend the meaning of what I see. This has happened to me before. Poetry has often made me see things anew. I remember the transforming moment of first reading R.S. Thomas's beautiful and visionary poem 'The Bright Field', how it revealed that the suddenly illuminated small field shining in your own landscape is, to the creative artist,

> *the pearl*
>
> *of great price, the one field that had*
>
> *the treasure in it.*

The poet continues: 'It is the turning/aside like Moses to the miracle/of the lit bush.'

R.S. Thomas is not the only poet to use the image of the burning bush to show the transforming power of the moment of creative inspiration. In *A Pilgrim at Tinker Creek*, Annie Dillard gives several examples of the electrifying vision experienced by the artist. All a poet can do, as Annie Dillard says, is be there. That day I saw the hill country in new colours, its mythology and geology made manifest in paint through the painter's eye, just as I had understood that a rape field is a spiritual matter when R.S. showed me.

Mary and I have often talked of the connection between painting and words, and of our cultural influences. Landscape is a book, and there is more to it than meets the eye. Mary's work uses her country's languages, literature, history, graffiti, slogans and banners. That I was writing about the rich and layered story of Llyn y Fan Fach and Mary was painting it is no coincidence. It is a common cultural source. We had often talked of the place and its legend, and in the winter of 1999-2000 we began to exchange ideas and work-in-progress. In her studio were many watercolour sketches and a large painting of the lake, still in progress. We exchanged versions of the story. I had sent her my own work-in-progress on Llyn y Fan, and a sequence of poems written for the National Botanic Garden of Wales, not far from Myddfai and the landscape of the story. Part of this sequence dealt with geological eras. The theme excited Mary. She scored her painting of Llyn y Fan with rock strata and graffiti from the poems, Stone Age symbols and remedies from the Physicians of Myddfai. Both of us were digging deep for the meaning of a landscape. It would have been a journey into the dark but for the humanity of an old sad story.

Llyn y Fan Fach lies under the Carmarthen Fans, and is associated with the story of the girl from the lake who mothered the tribe of healers and botanists from whom the Physicians of Myddfai were descended. Archaeologists guess that the story is rooted in the time when the Iron Age Celts began to arrive in Britain. The archaeological clue is iron. If the mortal husband strikes his lake-girl wife three times with iron she must return to the lake. The Stone Age people knew no metal. It was the Bronze and especially the Iron Age that brought to Britain the craft of forging metal, and the Celts who made art out of it. The three strikes of iron are omitted from some versions of the Llyn y Fan story, though my father, born and brought up in Carmarthenshire, always included it in his telling of it. Just to know the legend and to look at the landscape tells us what it means. The page of still water. The mountain's book. The strata that took all time to lay down. The brief episodes of turmoil that crumpled and folded and opened it to view. The story is there, in the strata, in the graffiti, in the legend, the stuff of art and poetry.

Shape-shifting with every generation, myth encapsulates the imaginative history of a culture that parallels its factual history. Together they make an illuminated manuscript, a painting of the past. The lake is real enough, but who was the girl who came from its depths? Who was her lover on the shore? Why was she afraid of iron? Why at its third touch does she return to the lake forever? What does it all mean?

Myth melts into history. The lake took back the Stone Age girl and her people, as it would take the Iron Age and all else that went before us. The landscape is the past. That is the story's meaning. Knowing the story, knowing what has made her people who they are is the stuff of the work, and the force that makes it art is a matter of transformation, a turning aside to the lit bush.

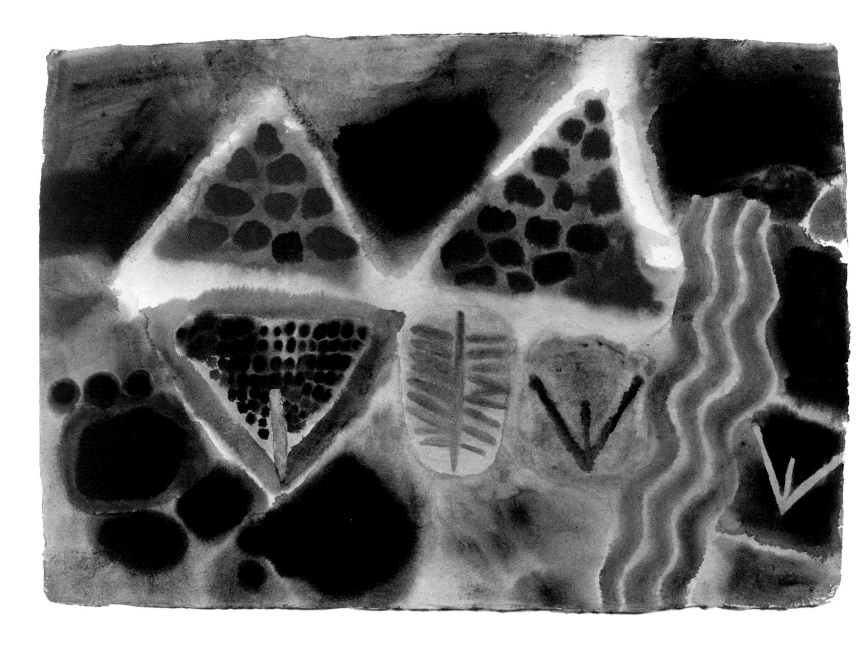

Germination

The Physicians of Myddfai

LLYN Y FAN FACH

Like a bowl of milk
the mountain cups the lake
deep and dark as the past,
and history's lost
where the Ages of Stone,
Bronze and Iron left their bones
under the earth, under the water
with the lake king's daughter.

Look into that surface.
It's not your face
you see, but hers,
as the wind stirs
water's mirror.
Wind turns history's
pages, each leaf
not yours but a people's grief.

LISTENING

What do the children say
when they've gazed into the story
playing itself in their hearts
in the quiet of the classroom,
in the quiet of a voice reading
and pages turning?
When the book is closed
they're silent at the mystery of loss.

Then Joe says: It's not twins.
It's a girl and her reflection.
Bethan says: She's the Stone Age.
He's the Iron Age.
Emma says: The lake is death.
David says: The lake is the past.
Manon says: It's true then.
Then they're silent at the hurt of it.

CHOOSING

The ages drown, dissolved into the past,
our island stories lie half lost
in archaeology, the myths and silts
of ancient settlements.

With his mother's bread he won her from the lake,
three loaves, three chances for love to break
the boundaries of earth and water, to crack
time and the elements.

Three strikes of metal and she was gone.
Three sons were born of that union
of Stone Age and Celt, of stone and iron,
of earth-skills and art.

Their inheritance: their father's grief,
their mother's way with herbs, with root and leaf,
the distillations of plants to bring relief
to body and heart.

HEALING

Linctus, cordials, electuaries, quoils,
conserves of borage, bugloss and burdock,
scurvy grass, cowslip, wormwood, rue.

The sons of the sons of the sons
of the woman of water
and the man of the earth,
carried the art of healing
down the generations,
as if the human mind
were an amphora of precious oils
that must never be spilt.

Bittersweet, dove's foot, nailwort, thorough wax,
hemlock, tamarisk, colt's foot, thornberry,
heartsease, honeysuckle, calamint, camomile.

History's blurred with legend,
but the physicians' names
are on the graves at Myddfai,
their secrets buried with their bones.
Their place was a safe house
for wild and tame, the otter's home,
black oil sleeking the night river
leaving its sprent on the stones.

Snakeweed, angelica, periwinkle, balm,
adders tongue, betony, bugle, burnet,
crowsfoot, henbane, watercress, sorrel.

From them we might have learned
the healing balm of plants.
Will this be the day they loose
the furious gene, trampling
the heal-all that grows secretly
in a field singing with bees,
that might have given us what science
seeks in its test-tubes and trays?

Tormentil, woundwort, plantain, dock,
comfrey, horsetail, briony, scabious,
hyssop, mallow, mustard, mint.

SEEING

She dips her brush in sky,
in rain, in mythology,
and comes up with who we are.

The brush unloads its cloud
in a jar to take its place
with stratocumulus,

a thunder-head to the south,
a trace of Western rose in cirrus
like pulled fleece on the Fan,

a front off the Atlantic
hitting high ground before
precipitation.

Llyn y Fan I

101

She paints with rain. A slab
of sunlight. A field dry-edged with walls.
All the colours of light.

Here at the lake, and later
in her schoolroom studio,
the paint-tubes' poetry

is a remembered litany,
rose and purple madder, umber, crimson,
ochre and gold and cerulean blue,

Even white is a prism.
Even black is reached
through the rainbow's narrowing tunnel.

BELIEVING

A Stone Age hand in umber on a wall
gesturing with cave-beasts, symbols and script,
and the woman-sign, the vulva's triangle,
the cup of blood, of pearl-seed.

Print of hoof, hand, paw, foot,
clawed, cloven, chiselled, calcified.
Suddenly we hear the heartbeat and breath
of a living beast, of a man,

or a woman calling from so long ago
we can believe she stood by tallow-light
to make her mark here on the cave's page,
dipping her hand in blood.

Gillian Clarke

Llyn y Fan II

103

... pre-Cambrian, Phanerozoic,

chaptered with eras,

paragraphed with epochs, ages, chrons,

sedimentary time

laid down and shaped

with the patience of stone ...

from 'Earth Story' by Gillian Clarke

opposite Black Gold

'. . . from the tropical swamps/that made the coal your fathers cut . . .'

from 'Earth Story' by Gillian Clarke

Age Lines

STUDIES THE WORK GROWS FROM LINE DRAWINGS AND COLOUR NOTES MADE OUT IN THE LANDSCAPE WHICH ARE SUBSEQUENTLY DEVELOPED INTO SMALL COLOUR STUDIES OF 8" X 10" IN THE STUDIO. MANY OF THESE STUDIES ARE DISCARDED, BUT THOSE WHICH ARE PROMISING BECOME WORKS ON A LARGER SCALE ON PAPER OR ON CANVAS.

Studies 3, 4, 5

Studies 6, 7, 8, 9

Indigo and Purple Madder *Mary Lloyd Jones*

When we consider what I call the satellite culture, we find two reasons against consenting to its complete absorption into the stronger culture. The first objection is one so profound that it must simply be accepted; it is the instinct of every living thing to persist in its own being... It would be no gain whatsoever for English culture for the Welsh, Scots and Irish to become indistinguishable from Englishmen – what would happen of course, is that we should all become indistinguishable featureless Britons at a lower level of culture than that of any of the separate regions.

T.S. Eliot, *Notes towards the Definition of Culture* (Faber & Faber 1948)

During the five years I spent at Cardiff College of Art in the early fifties I only ever encountered two or three other students who could speak Welsh. Most of my fellow students came from the industrial valleys, a large proportion commuting each day and disappearing at weekends. I therefore became accustomed very quickly to being a member of a minority. I was in fact a foreigner in my own capital city. My upbringing in a tiny, scattered village in the uplands of Ceredigion had been totally different from that of the other students who only knew urban living. The journey from Devil's Bridge to Cardiff on the Western Welsh bus took all day. And during those ten hours I had time to orientate myself, so that I could slide with ease between two worlds.

The benefits of industrialisation in the form of mains electricity and mains water did not arrive in Devil's Bridge

Ponterwyd

until the mid-fifties. What at the time seemed to be a distinct disadvantage did give me the benefit of experiences associated with rural peasant life never to be known by those who lived only in cities. Today I realise that I am one of the tiny and privileged minority who spent their formative years following a way of life that has remained virtually unchanged for thousands of years. Who can know the assault on the senses of the inky cold black of a winter's night in the country if they are accustomed only to street lights?

Very few children lived within playing distance, so I spent a great deal of time on my own. I grew to know intimately the square mile around my home. Long days were spent scrambling around the deep valley sides surrounding Devil's Bridge, covering territory that was quite dangerous, but I grew to know the chasms and waterfalls and could navigate the terrain in safety. This extensive knowledge of a particular place now informs my work, and images set in the experience of this time now emerge with a life of their own in my paintings.

My father never missed a weather forecast even in old age, a habit, I believe, inherited from generations of forefathers whose existence depended on responding to the weather. My father also inherited the ancient art of the *cyfarwydd* (storyteller); neighbours would gather on winter nights to listen to his endless repertoire of tales from the recent past of minor catastrophes, comic characters and amusing incidents. Some of these stories dealt with darker material, tales of corpse candles associated with particular places and the astonishing skills of the *cwnjer* (conjurer) who could undo spells and curses and cure burns at great distances. Through these stories I glimpsed an older world that was mysterious and irrational. These tales cemented a permanent relationship and sense of belonging to the village and its environs.

To this day I cannot explain what gave me the idea that I would be an artist. I had no role models within my family, school, or even my community. Indeed, I did not meet a real live artist before entering college. During my school years in Aberystwyth I only remember seeing one exhibition of contemporary art which was at the National Library, in those days the only venue in west Wales which had an art gallery. But drawing and reading were constant activities and gradually the need to enter that place created by my own marks became an essential part of me.[1]

'Perhaps what one wants to say is formed in childhood and the rest of one's life is spent trying to say it,' wrote

Barbara Hepworth. This is a theory that seems particularly relevant to my own development as an artist. The path towards a visual language that could express what I want to say has taken many wrong turnings and ended up down more than a few cul-de-sacs in the past, but certain themes have prevailed. Those who have followed my work will have noticed, for example, that my landscapes are frequently ripped and torn, and breaks and folds appear unexpectedly, indicating a threatened countryside and an unstable situation. I have also used fabrics in many different ways, often dyeing and stretching material. The folding, pleating, twisting, ripping, wiping and hanging of fabric are all activities strongly connected with domesticity. However, I have avoided the boredom usually associated with such domestic tasks by using them to articulate a new artistic vocabulary. Today, I endeavour constantly to create and re-create fresh configurations of this work.

Experiences outside Wales have provided key stages in the development of a personal language. Seeing the carved rocks on Rombalds Moor in Yorkshire inspired me to incorporate man-made marks into a landscape, for example. This led to an ongoing interest in the beginnings of language and early alphabets. The Ogham alphabet and Coelbren, the Bardic Alphabet, were secret languages restricted to small groups of initiates. Using these alphabets to suggest unexpected readings in my paintings provides an ambiguity which I find satisfying. That oblique references to otherness, to a Welsh identity, can be made in this way seemed to be appropriate.

My journeys to India have enabled me to immerse myself in a culture where the use of colour is sophisticated and part of everyone's heritage. One of my aims was to increase my fluency in the orchestration of colour, something that could enrich my work on returning home. Here in the West, artists continue to live on the margins of society, so it was a great joy to be in a culture where everyone was an artist, where women painted elaborate designs on the ground and around doorways for special festivals, not for profit, but as a gift for the family and the community. The experience of fields of colour, miles of cloth on structures hanging to dry in the sun and stretched out on the ground like flowerbeds, continues to inform my work.

An intimate relationship with the land is common to all indigenous peoples. For a European learning about the

Autumn Light

113

attitudes and practices of American Indians and Australian Aborigines, the loss resulting from the destruction of these cultures is a tragedy for our time and for future generations. For the Australian Aborigines, painting was an integral part of life, like walking and sleeping. It was the painting process that re-affirmed their links and sense of rootedness in the landscape.

Achieving an understanding of my own creative process has been a solitary and often painful task but I have been helped by some key writers like Anton Ehrenzweig in his book, *The Hidden Order of Art*.[2] The first requirement is secure blocks of uninterrupted time: a minimum of three consecutive days which enable one to live and sleep and be completely immersed in the work. It is only then that a flash of inspiration, a joyful surprise can happen. The second requirement is a supportive presence, a mentor who will provide encouragement, practical help and a belief in the value of one's endeavours. That support has been provided by my husband, John.

The initial urge to begin a series of works always follows being out in a big space experiencing solitude and emptiness, weather and wilderness and this is why I am a landscape painter. In our culture, the rural is associated with backwardness, so by painting the rural as opposed to the urban, one is in danger of being swamped by the opposing tide. Using colour as a musical language I try to sing the landscape. It is through paint that the language of colour can be best explored and this is why, in the face of the general rejection of mainstream art, I remain committed to the art of painting.

The process of painting is like a high wire act. With every movement or brushstroke the tension increases. The process is full of risk, but without risk, nothing is achieved. Painting is a difficult art, which is why painters often do their best work in old age. I try to maintain spontaneity; I aim to make the final work look as though it was easy and unforced. Intuition must be exercised; rational decisions must also be made. Painting is a ballet, dancing with hand and brush, changing rhythms… the best marks arrive as a complete surprise. An artist's role is to behold, to offer those who care to look a new pair of eyes. A painting can accommodate paradox: whilst dealing with damage, my hope is that a painting can, at the same time, demonstrate the land's capacity for healing and regeneration.

Within my lifetime the climate for the visual arts in Wales has improved dramatically, particularly in recent years, when research funding has enabled art historians to reclaim a lost visual culture. We now have an army of young Welsh artists, both women and men, who are choosing to stay in Wales and their work is contributing to a living culture. The great numbers of artists moving into Wales from elsewhere constantly swell the ranks of this native army. These newcomers can rapidly engage with and contribute to the culture, as a visual language has no barriers. Exhibitions and festivals pop up in vestries, village halls and arts centres all over rural Wales, generating much positive energy. The arrival of the Welsh Assembly has changed the climate and certainly contributes to the feelings of hope that Wales might be on the brink of a great flowering of the visual arts.

In spite of this surge of energy, Wales continues to lack basic institutions that can support and develop the potential that undoubtedly exists. We lack a National Gallery of Contemporary Art, for example, and a gallery to house the History of Welsh Visual Culture. In the future, cultural exchanges with the devolved regions of Britain and with small nations in the rest of Europe would enable Welsh art to emerge from the margins and enrich the culture of Britain. It would be a significant step forward and, no doubt, would please the spirit of T.S. Eliot.

[1] The opening five paragraphs of this essay are taken from *Our Sisters Land: The Changing Identities of Women in Wales* (University of Wales Press, 1994).
[2] Anton Ehrenzweig, *The Hidden Order of Art* (Weidenfeld and Nicholson, 1967).

Biographical Notes

1993   *Dyfed Art Show* (selector George Melly), Oriel Myrddin and Carmarthen Library Gallery
Designs for Gasometer, Cywaith Cymru/Artworks Wales
The Land and Sea, Oriel Myrddin and Carmarthen Museum
Bath Art Fair, represented by the Martin Tinney Gallery
Mixed Feelings, Dean Clough Gallery, Halifax
Celtic Landscape, Gallery of Modern Art, London
Art for Sale/Guardian Newspaper: work selected for November

1993   *Landscape Exhibition,* Anthony Hepworth Fine Art, Bath

1992   *International Art Fair,* Miami, U.S.A.; represented by Sweet Waters Gallery, London
Twentieth Century British Art Fair; represented by Sweet Waters Gallery, London and Ogle Fine Art, Cheltenham
Bath and Edinburgh Art Fairs; represented by Martin Tinney Gallery
Wales Open Exhibition, Aberystwyth Arts Centre
Art for Sale/Guardian Newspaper Exhibitions, Whiteley's, London
Symbolic Elements in Landscape Painting, Sweet Waters Gallery, London.

1991   *Welsh Contemporaries,* Red Square Gallery, London
Wales Open Exhibition, Aberystwyth Arts Centre
Blue Point Gallery, Berlin
Safleoedd/Sites, Artworks Wales/Cywaith Cymru, The Old Library, Cardiff
Ogle Fine Art, Cheltenham
Twentieth Century British Art Fair, Royal College of Art, London; represented by Ogle Fine Art, Cheltenham and Sweet Waters Gallery, London
Mercia Fine Art/Contemporary Art at the Shire Hall, Newport

1991   *Recent works* (with Sue Hunt and Jacqueline Alkema), West Wharf Gallery, Cardiff

1990   Pelter Sands Gallery, Bristol
St David's Day Exhibition, The Old School, Lisvane, Cardiff
Dyfed Art Show (selector Terry Frost)
Solo Express, Group Show, Monserrat Gallery, New York
Katherine Starr Gallery, Philadelphia and Rosenfeld Gallery, Philadelphia
The Rhymney Valley Royal National Eisteddfod Exhibition, curated by Cen Williams
Wales Open Exhibition, Aberystwyth Arts Centre

Wales' First Art Fair, represented by the Power House Gallery, Laugharne
The Old School Gallery, Lisvane, Cardiff, curated by Cen Williams
The Painted Chair, Kilvert Gallery Christmas Show, Clyro, Powys
Save St David's, touring exhibition at St Mary's Hall, St. David's, the West Wharf Gallery, Cardiff and the Vanessa Deveraux Gallery, London
The Wales/Philadelphia Visual Arts Exchange Exhibition (with Kathy Quigley of Philadelphia) at West Wharf Gallery, Cardiff

PRIZES AND COMMISSIONS

2000   Contemporary Art Society for Wales; selected Artist for Millennium Print Project

1997   Artist's Development Grant, Arts Council of Wales, towards cost of Residency in Centre D'Art i Natura di Farrera, Catalunya

1996   Design of Commemorative Plate for Urdd National Eisteddfod, Lampeter, 1999

1997   Travel Grant, Arts Council of Wales

1996   First prize, *Wales Open Exhibition,* Aberystwyth Arts Centre

1992   *Earth Words Project*; collaboration with the poet Janet Dubé for the Garden Festival, Ebbw Vale , 1992

ARTICLES AND PUBLICATIONS

BOOKS DEVOTED TO THE ARTIST

2001   *The Colour of Saying,* ed. Eve Ropek, Gomer Press/Aberystwyth Arts Centre

BOOKS INCLUDING CHAPTERS ON THE ARTIST

2000   *Darllen Delweddau, Beirdd ac Artistiaid,* ed. Iwan Bala, Gwasg Carreg Gwalch

1999   *Certain Welsh Artists,* ed. Iwan Bala, Seren Books.

1997   *Cymru Wrth eu Gwaith/Welsh People at Work,* Elin Meek, Y Lolfa

BOOK CHAPTERS AND ARTICLES BY THE ARTIST

2000   *Taliesin* (108), review of *Darganfod Celf Cymru,* ed. Ivor Davies and Ceridwen Lloyd-Morgan, University of Wales Press

1998 *Planet* (139), article on her residency at the Centre d'Art i
       Natura de Farrera in Catalunya
1995 'Between Two Worlds', in *Our Sisters' Land: The Changing
       Identities of Women in Wales*, ed. Jane Aaron, Sandra Betts,
       Teresa Rees and Moira Vincintelli, University of Wales
       Press

ARTICLES ON THE ARTIST
1997 Norbert Lynton, essay for *Shared Language* catalogue
1996 'From Perspective to Paradise', Peter Abbs, *Resurgence* (17)
1993 Robin Tomos, *Golwg*, April 1993
1991 Derek Hyatt, essay for *First Language* exhibition catalogue
       for Aberystwyth Arts Centre
       Menna Baines, article on *First Language* exhibition, *Golwg*,
       25 April 1991
       Nigel Jenkins, *Planet* (88), profile of Mary Lloyd Jones
       Jill Piercy, essay for *Recent Work* exhibition catalogue,
       Rhondda Heritage Park
       D. Guaranga, essay for *Recent Work* exhibition catalogue,
       Sweet Waters Gallery, London
       Review by Siân Wyn Jones, *Y Faner*, 25 October 1991 at the
       Sweet Waters gallery, London
       Modern Painters, Autumn 1991 [colour illustration on
       gallery page]

OTHER ACTIVITIES

MISCELLANEOUS
1994 Dewi Prys Thomas Memorial Lecture, Royal National
       Eisteddfod, Neath
1993 Member of the Selection Panel for the Art and Craft
       Exhibition, Royal National Eisteddfod, Builth Wells
1991 Member of the Selection Panel for the Fine Art Exhibition,
       Royal National Eisteddfod, Bro Delyn
1988 Residency at The Tyrone Guthrie Centre, Annaghmakerig,
       Ireland

TELEVISION
2001 In conversation with naturalist Iolo Williams on the S4C
       programme *Crwydro* (Telesgôp)
2000 Interview on the river Rheidol with David Petersen for the
       HTV series *River Patrol*

1998 Item on exhibition at Oglivy and Estill, presented by Mal
       Pope, *Y Sioe Gelf* (Cwmni Da, for S4C)
       Item on exhibition at Oglivy and Estill, *Primetime*, HTV
1997 Item on the journey to India, *Y Sioe Gelf*
1994 'Three Welsh Landscape Painters', *Primetime*, HTV
       Film of the New York Exhibition at the Monserrat Gallery
       for *Hel Straeon*, S4C
1993 Item on Martin Tinney Gallery exhibition, *Primetime*, HTV
       Film of work in studio and in the Martin Tinney Gallery,
       Cardiff, *Heno*, S4C
       Interview for item on the National Museum of Wales,
       The Slate, BBC 1 Wales
       Item on the Highland Exchange residency, *The Slate*, BBC 1
       Wales
1991 Item on *First Language* exhibition for *Primetime*, HTV
1990 'Graffiti', S4C
       Film of the Wales/Philadelphia Exchange of work by Kathy
       Quigley and Mary Lloyd Jones, seen in the Aberbanc
       Studios, *Scene at 6*, HTV

PUBLIC COLLECTIONS

Alquin College, York
  University
Arts Council of Wales
BBC Wales
Carmarthenshire County
  Council
Ceredigion County Council
Cite Di Adria Collection
Clwyd County Council
Contemporary Art Society for
  Wales
Crawford Museum and Gallery,
  Cork, Ireland
Green Mountain College,
  Vermont

Highland Regional Council
Keele University
Museum of Modern Art, Wales,
  Machynlleth
National Library of Wales
National Museum of Wales
S4C
The Cardiff Arena/World Trade
  Centre
The Tyrone Guthrie Centre,
  Ireland
University of Wales, Bangor
University of Wales, Lampeter
Wrexham Arts Centre

Notes on the contributors

PETER ABBS is a founding member of New Metaphysical Art – a movement committed to radical new developments in the making and understanding of art. Recent publications include *The Polemics of Imagination* and *Love after Sappho*. He is Professor of Arts Education at Sussex and directs the MA in Creative Writing.

GILLIAN CLARKE is a poet and a playwright, whose work is studied by school students and has been translated into ten languages. She is President of Tŷ Newydd, the Writers' Centre in north Wales which she helped to found, and is a tutor on the creative writing course at the University of Glamorgan.

DEREK HYATT is an artist and a writer, and a Companion of the Guild of St. George, founded by John Ruskin to 'promote education and appreciation in the arts'. He has exhibited widely and is a regular contributor to arts publications, including *Modern Painters*.

NIGEL JENKINS is a Swansea-based poet, writer and lecturer, one of Wales's 'foremost wordsmiths' and an acclaimed performer of his work. He has published both poetry and prose, including the volumes *Ambush* and *Gwalia in Khasia*. In 1995 he was awarded the Arts Council of Wales Book of the Year award for *Gwalia in Khasia*.

EVE ROPEK is exhibitions organiser at Aberystwyth Arts Centre, curating a programme of contemporary art and craft within the Centre's galleries which includes the spacious new Gallery 1, part of the recent Lottery-funded development designed by the architect Peter Roberts. She has edited many contemporary art catalogues in recent years, including 'Luminaries', 'The Cat Scratched little Johnny' and 'The American Way'.

MARY SARA is a freelance art critic, writer and curator, and is the co-ordinator of Open House adult education at Harewood House, Yorkshire. She has written extensively on art and artists, including catalogue essays on Craigie Aitchison, Norman Ackroyd and Victoria Crowe, and she curated 'St Ives artists and their friends in the North'.

An earlier version of 'Singing the Landscape' by Nigel Jenkins appeared in *Planet* 88 (1991). 'First Language' by Derek Hyatt was first published by Aberystwyth Arts Centre (1990).

Details of works